AMERICAN DOCUMENTS

The Declaration *of* Independence

Thomas Jefferson

Judith Lloyd Yero

Picture Credits

Cover (flag) Rubberball Productions/Getty Images; cover (document), pages 7, 19 (bottom) Joseph Sohm/Corbis; cover (bell), 19 (right) Independence National Historic Park Collection; pages 1, 10 The Granger Collection, New York; page 2-3 Dick Frank/Corbis; page 4 Stone/Getty Images; page 4-5 Wally McNamee/Corbis; pages 6, 17, 19 (left), 24 Bettmann/Corbis; page 9 Historical Society of Pennsylvania; pages 9, 15 (top), 25 (right) Louis. S. Glanzman/National Geographic Image Collection; page 11 (top) Corbis; page 11 (bottom left) Colonial Williamsburg Foundation; page 11 (right) Quadrillion/Corbis; page 12 (top) Massachusetts Historical Society; pages 12 (bottom), 16, 19 (middle), 25 (left), 27 (top left) Courtesy of the Library of Congress; pages 12-13, 13, 18, 27 (top right) Hulton | Archive/Getty Images; pages 14-15 Burstein Collection/Corbis; page 20-21 Connecticut State Historical Society; Hartford, CT; pages 22-23 New York Historical Society; page 26 Washington and Lee University; pages 26-27 The Senate of the Commonwealth of Virginia; Courtesy of the Library of Virginia; page 28 (right) Flip Schulke/Corbis; page 28 (left) United States Postal Service; page 29 Leif Skoogfors/Corbis; page 30 Joseph Sohm/Visions of America/Corbis; page 31 Scott T. Smith/Corbis.

Produced through the worldwide resources of the National Geographic Society, John M. Fahey, Jr., President and Chief Executive Officer; Gilbert M. Grosvenor, Chairman of the Board; Nina D. Hoffman, Executive Vice President and President, Books and Education Publishing Group.

Prepared by National Geographic School Publishing and Children s Books

Ericka Markman, Senior Vice President and President, Children's Books and Education Publishing Group; Steve Mico, Vice President, Editorial Director; Marianne Hiland, Executive Editor; Anita Schwartz, Project Editor, Suzanne Patrick Fonda, Children's Books Project Editor; Jim Hiscott, Design Manager; Kristin Hanneman, Illustrations Manager; Diana Bourdrez, Picture Editor; Matt Wascavage, Manager of Publishing Services; Sean Philpotts, Production Manager.

Manufacturing and Quality Management

Christopher A. Liedel, Chief Financial Officer; Phillip L. Schlosser, Director; Clifton M. Brown, Manager.

Consultants/Reviewers

Dr. Margit E. McGuire, School of Education, Seattle University, Seattle, Washington

Dr. Paul Finkelman, Chapman Distinguished Professor of Law, University of Tulsa Law School, Tulsa, Oklahoma

Book Development

Nieman, Inc.

Book Design

Steven Curtis Design, Inc.

Art Direction

Dan Banks, Project Design Company

Photo Research

Corrine L. Brock, In the Lupe, Inc.

ISBN 0-7922-5397-3 (hardcover)

ISBN 0-7922-5398-1 (library binding)

Previously published as *Documents of Freedom: The Declaration of Independence* (National Geographic Reading Expeditions). Copyright © 2004
ISBN 0-7922-4554-7 (paperback)

Published by the NATIONAL GEOGRAPHIC SOCIETY
1145 17th Street, N.W.
Washington, D.C. 20036-4688

Printed in the U.S.A.

Table of Contents

Introduction

What if the people of your country were ruled by an unjust king who told you what to do? When you complained, he sent soldiers to make you obey. Would you want to do something about this? In 1776, Americans faced this problem, and they did something about it. They got rid of the king who ruled them and started to rule themselves. These Americans wanted to make sure that everyone understood what they were doing and why they were doing it. So they wrote the Declaration of Independence.

Americans register to vote so they can have a voice in how our country is run.

Those who wrote the Declaration said some very startling things. They said that people had certain basic rights that no ruler could take away. They said that rulers have a right to govern only as long as the people freely give them the power to do so. They said that when the people decide to take that power away, they can do it. These were big claims in 1776, and they still are today.

What events led to the Declaration of Independence? What does the document say? What influence has the Declaration had on history? How does it affect us today? Let's find out.

Every four years, Americans hold political conventions to choose candidates for President and Vice President.

On Display

During the Revolution, the signed copy of the Declaration moved from one place to another. Today, the Declaration sits in a special case at the National Archives in Washington, D.C.

Original Document

The original Declaration of Independence was written in ink on a sheet of parchment $24\frac{1}{4}$ inches wide and $29\frac{3}{4}$ inches long. Years of rolling and unrolling caused a lot of damage to the paper and ink. Exposure to light faded the ink even more. Today, special lighting prevents more fading of the ink.

North to South

Signers from the northernmost state, New Hampshire, wrote their names first. Those from Georgia, the southernmost state, signed last.

Youngest and Oldest

The youngest signer was Edward Rutledge of South Carolina, who was 26. The oldest was 70-year-old Benjamin Franklin.

...We hold these truths to be self-evident, that all men are created equal, that they are endowed by their Creator with certain unalienable Rights, that among these are Life, Liberty, and the pursuit of Happiness...

Visitors view the Declaration of Independence at the National Archives.

IN CONGRESS, JULY 4, 1776.

The unanimous Declaration of the thirteen united States of America.

Road to Freedom

Wealth! Power! Control of trade! Like other countries in Europe, Britain wanted power. So it created colonies.

★

The Business of Colonies

A **colony** is a region ruled by another country. Britain's American colonies were valuable sources of raw materials. For example, the American colonies had large deposits of iron ore. During the early 1700s, Americans greatly increased their production of raw iron. Britain would not let the colonists make finished iron goods. Britain wanted to protect its own iron industry. So, Americans were forced to buy British iron goods.

Britain wanted to control the economies of the colonies.

Colonies are also important as markets. The ruling country sells its goods there. Britain sold the American colonists many products, such as glass, china, silverware, and guns. Over time, the colonists were able to make these things for themselves. Often Britain told the colonists no. They must buy British goods.

Americans and Self-Government

The colonists were British **subjects,** people under the authority of a king. They also had the right to govern themselves, as long as they obeyed British law. As in Britain, male colonists who owned land could vote. They elected colonial **assemblies** to make laws. Many leaders of the American Revolution—including Thomas Jefferson, John Adams, and Benjamin Franklin—got their start in these assemblies.

The king had the last word. He could **veto,** or reject, the laws that the assemblies passed. That seldom happened, but King George III had that power.

For many colonies, the king appointed a **royal governor.** The colonists didn't elect him. He represented the king, and he had the final say on laws made by the assembly. He could shut down the assembly if he wanted, but the assembly controlled the tax money it raised. It could refuse to give the governor funds—even cut off his salary!

The colonists got used to making their own laws. Then, when Britain passed new laws that affected their lives, the colonists objected.

Members of the Virginia assembly debate how to respond to new British laws.

A War and Taxes

Britain and France both had colonies in North America. Between 1754 and 1763, they fought a war for control of North America. Because the French were aided by some Native American peoples, this conflict is called the French and Indian War. George Washington was a young officer in this war. He fought side by side with British soldiers and gained experience in leading troops. In the end, Britain and the colonists won. Britain took over French lands and nearly doubled the size of its American colonies.

Then came a new set of problems for Britain's King George III. The colonists were his subjects, but so were the Native Americans. The two groups were not getting along.

George Washington, fighting for Britain against the French, tips his hat to the British flag.

Native Americans attacked the colonists when they moved into the lands beyond the Appalachian Mountains. To keep the peace, the king said in 1763 that the colonists could not live west of the mountains. He ordered the settlers who were already there to return east. The colonists did not like the king's order. Hadn't they just fought a war for the right to settle that land?

Colonists fought Native Americans in frontier areas beyond the Appalachian Mountains.

Also, fighting the war had cost a great deal of money. King George III decided that since the war was about defending the colonies, the Americans should pay some of its cost. The colonists already paid taxes to support their local governments. Now **Parliament**, Britain's lawmaking body, demanded money for the government in Britain. This was different!

The colonists couldn't elect members of Parliament. They had no say in these new taxes. The Americans believed this was wrong. Only lawmakers elected by the people had the right to tax them. A new cry went up. "No taxation without representation!"

King George III
George III just didn't get it! Early in his reign, the king ordered a new coach covered in gold. The cost today would be more than one million dollars! At about the same time, he claimed to be broke from defending the colonies.

More Taxes, More Trouble

In 1765, English lawmakers passed the Stamp Act. Do you want to read a newspaper? Buy a stamp. Do you want a marriage license? Buy a stamp. This law forced colonists to pay taxes on printed matter of all kinds. The colonists resisted. Colonial merchants agreed to not buy and sell English goods. Women joined this **boycott**. Who needs paper? We'll write on dried leaves.

Colonial assemblies met. They called the Stamp Act illegal. We had no voice in making the laws, they said, so we don't have to obey them! British merchants were hurt by the boycotts. They complained that no one was buying their goods. Parliament gave in and ended the Stamp Act in 1766.

Colonists burn tax stamps like the one shown here in an act of protest.

In the following years, the British imposed other taxes on the colonies. Some colonists became tired of words. They believed the time had come for action.

In Boston, Samuel Adams formed the Sons of Liberty to protest the taxes. Adams warned against violence, but some colonists didn't listen. One mob burned an image of a local tax collector.

In March 1770, protesters in Boston yelled threats and threw snowballs at a dozen British soldiers. When the frightened soldiers fired on them, five colonists died. The dead included 17-year-old Samuel Maverick and Crispus Attucks, a black sailor. Colonial newspapers called the shootings the "Boston Massacre."

There was more trouble in 1773, again in Boston. Before this time, colonial merchants had controlled the sale of tea. Now a new law gave that control to a British company. The colonists feared this meant higher prices for tea. In 1773, a group of colonists dressed up as Mohawk Indians. They boarded English ships docked in Boston Harbor and tossed 342 crates of tea into the sea. This was the famous "Boston Tea Party." The British government was outraged. British troops swarmed over Boston.

British soldiers fire on a crowd of colonists in the Boston Massacre.

Samuel Adams

A former tax collector became a fierce voice against "taxation without representation." Sam Adams was very good at getting people worked up about the British. They offered him money and a big job if he would quiet down. Although he was not a rich man, Adams refused.

First Battles with the British

When the British troops took over Boston, the colonists had
had enough! In 1774, leaders from 12 of the 13 colonies
met in Philadelphia. They called themselves the **Continental
Congress**. They sent a polite but firm statement to King
George. In it, they demanded the same rights as Englishmen.
The king ignored their demands. Instead, he sent more
British troops. The colonists, he said, were rebels.

The colonists prepared for war. They gathered weapons
and food. When the British came, they would be ready. On
April 18, 1775, 700 British troops marched out of Boston.

Thomas Paine

Thomas Paine arrived in America from Britain in 1774. It didn't take him long to point out one of the main problems with the British colonies in America. He said that it made no sense for a tiny island nation like Britain to rule a huge area like America.

Their goal was to capture the weapons the colonists had stored in nearby Concord. Word traveled quickly through the countryside—"The British are coming!"

The town of Lexington was on the way to Concord. Captain John Parker commanded the local colonial forces. He told his soldiers, "Stand your ground. Don't fire unless fired upon. But, if they want to have a war, let it begin here." And it did! Shots rang out. Americans were killed and wounded. The Revolutionary War had begun.

Many Americans still weren't sure if independence from Britain was right. Some argued that Britain had supported them and protected them. What would happen if they lost Britain's support?

In 1776, Thomas Paine wrote a pamphlet called *Common Sense*. Paine argued that America was great because of the hard work of its people. It didn't need Britain. Thousands of Americans read *Common Sense*. Paine's words—and a year of fighting—convinced many colonists that they no longer wanted the "rights of Englishmen." They wanted to be free Americans.

Writing the Declaration

The colonists would break their ties with Britain. They wanted the world to understand why they felt they had to take this serious step. They needed a formal statement that would explain their reasons.

On June 11, the Continental Congress picked a committee of five men to write a Declaration of Independence. Thomas Jefferson of Virginia and John Adams of Massachusetts got the most votes. Other members were Benjamin Franklin of Pennsylvania, Roger Sherman of Connecticut, and Robert Livingston of New York.

Who would actually put the words on paper? Adams wanted it to be Jefferson. He had three reasons. First, Jefferson's home state of Virginia was the oldest, biggest, and richest colony. Second, Adams, a very grumpy man at times, said that he himself was "unpopular." He didn't want people's feelings about him to affect how they reacted to the Declaration. Last, Adams said Jefferson was a "ten times better writer" than he was. Hidden away in his rented room, Jefferson struggled to put the American cause into strong, clear words. When he was finished, Adams and Franklin made only a few changes.

Detail of an early draft of the Declaration, showing edits

On July 2, 1776, the Continental Congress agreed to break away from Britain and King George. On July 4, after several more changes were made, the Declaration of Independence went to the printer.

The Drafting Committee

Benjamin Franklin

Writer, scientist, and statesman, Benjamin Franklin was probably the most famous American of his time. In addition to helping free his country, he invented bifocals and the lightning rod. He also built and played several musical instruments.

John Adams

On July 3, 1776, John Adams wrote his wife Abigail that he knew that the cost in "toil and blood and treasure" of winning freedom from Britain would be high. "Yet through all the gloom I can see the rays of [wonderful] light and glory. I can see that the end is more than worth all the means."

Thomas Jefferson

Jefferson ordered what was to be put on his tombstone. He wanted to be remembered for writing the Declaration of Independence and the Virginia Statute of Religious Freedom, and for founding the University of Virginia. He did not include being President of the United States among his achievements.

The Delegates Vote

The United States celebrates July 4 as Independence Day. In fact, delegates didn't sign the Declaration of Independence until about a month later. On July 4, delegates from 12 of the 13 colonies voted to adopt the Declaration. New York delegates waited for the entire New York assembly to see the document.

On July 5, delegates sent printed copies by horseback to the 13 colonial assemblies. By July 9, New York officially approved the Declaration. All 13 colonies had agreed to declare independence.

Congress prepared a handwritten copy of the Declaration. On August 2, 1776, delegates gathered around the table and signed their names. Signing the Declaration of Independence was an act of patriotism and courage. The signers were risking their lives. They were almost surely going to war with the world's greatest power. The Americans could very easily lose. If that happened, Britain would probably round up the signers and put them on trial. As Benjamin Franklin said, "We must all hang together or [certainly] we will all hang separately."

This famous painting of the adoption of the Declaration of Independence hangs in the Capitol in Washington, D.C.

The Signing

John Hancock

The president of the Continental Congress was the first to sign. John Hancock wrote his name in big, bold letters. He wanted to make sure that King George could read his name without his glasses! The British had already offered a reward for his capture. "Let them double their reward," he dared.

Caesar Rodney

In July 1776, Delaware's Caesar Rodney rode 80 miles by horseback to Philadelphia. He had skin cancer. By signing the Declaration, he gave up his chance to go to London for a possible cure. His country's freedom was more important.

John Dickinson

John Dickinson served in the Continental Congress and wrote many papers defending the rights of the colonists. He believed that Britain and the colonies could still settle their differences. So he refused to sign the Declaration of Independence.

A Closer Look

The Declaration of Independence has four parts. There is an introduction, a list of basic beliefs, a list of complaints, and a formal statement of independence.

★

The Preamble

The introduction, or **preamble** (PREE-am-buhl), is the first paragraph of the Declaration of Independence. In it, Jefferson tells what the purpose of the document is. He explains that Americans want the world to understand why they are breaking their ties with Britain. The document will explain what they believe. It will also list all of the events that have led them to take this action.

"a decent respect to the opinions of mankind requires…"

The colonists believed that the rest of the world deserved to understand why they were declaring their independence from Britain.

Basic Beliefs

Next, Jefferson explains what Americans believe about human rights and why people create governments. He begins by saying that anyone should be able to see that these beliefs are true.

What are the basic human rights? "All men are created equal." Everyone has the right to "life, liberty, and the pursuit of happiness." These basic rights are **unalienable.** That means no one can take them away—not even the British king.

Why do people create governments? Governments exist to protect basic human rights. The power of governments comes from the people. Rulers sometimes forget they are supposed to serve the people. They treat them unfairly and pass laws that the people didn't agree to. When that happens, the people have the right to change their government or just get rid of it. Then, they can set up a new government that will serve them better.

"All men are created equal"

"Equal" doesn't mean that everyone is the same. It means that every person has the right to the same treatment under the law. Whether they are born rich or poor, people have the right to be treated equally.

British troops burned the home of Richard Stockton, one of the signers of the Declaration of Independence. Such acts convinced many Americans it was time to change their government.

Complaints Against the King

Just accusing Britain of being unfair wasn't enough. The Continental Congress wanted to prove it to the world. The delegates wanted Americans to remember everything King George and Parliament had done wrong. What better way than to list the abuses and injuries the colonists had suffered? The list contains 27 offenses. Each one begins with the words, "He has," and then states some injustice the king had done. Here are some of the most important:

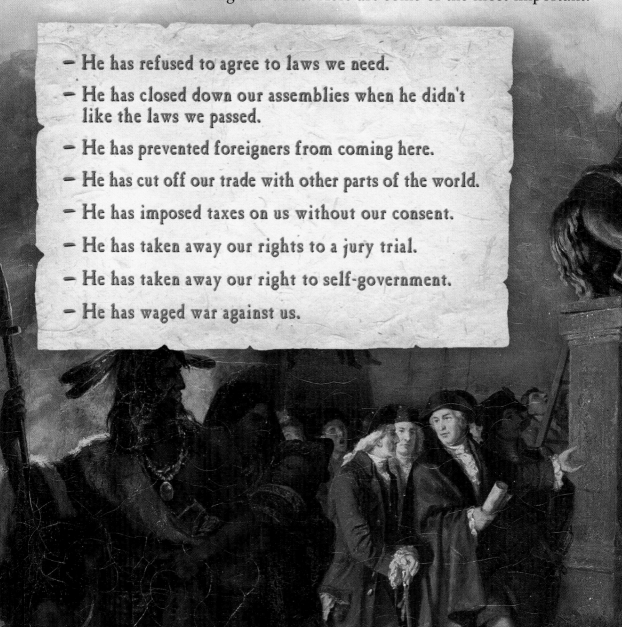

- He has refused to agree to laws we need.
- He has closed down our assemblies when he didn't like the laws we passed.
- He has prevented foreigners from coming here.
- He has cut off our trade with other parts of the world.
- He has imposed taxes on us without our consent.
- He has taken away our rights to a jury trial.
- He has taken away our right to self-government.
- He has waged war against us.

After reading the list, how could anyone disagree that King George was a cruel and unjust ruler, a **tyrant**? Such a person, said the Declaration of Independence, "is unfit to be the ruler of a free people."

The Statement of Independence

The Declaration ends by formally breaking the ties between the former colonies and Britain. These "Free and Independent States" now have the same powers of any other free state in the world.

"The Consent of the Governed"

Jefferson took this idea—that people give their government the right to rule them—from earlier European thinkers. It is the basis of modern democratic government.

Colonists showed their changed feelings about King George III by pulling down statues of him.

3

Winning Freedom

Printed copies of the Declaration of Independence spread like wildfire through the colonies.

★

What Happened Next

The sight of the Declaration thrilled many **Patriots,** colonists who supported independence. They posted copies in public places. They shouted the words from the steps of public buildings. Church bells rang out the news. Colonists sang and danced around bonfires. On July 9, General Washington had the Declaration read to his troops in New York.

American soldiers hear the Declaration of Independence.

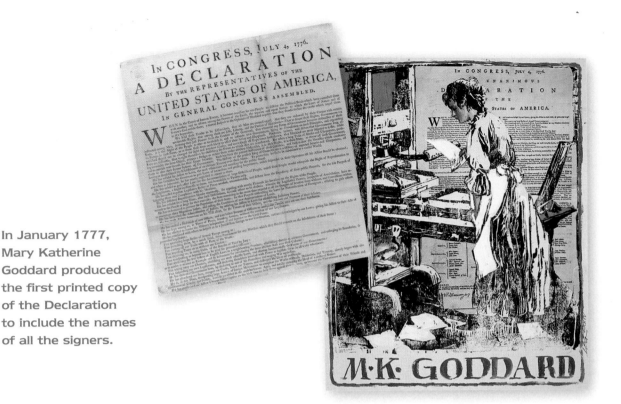

In January 1777, Mary Katherine Goddard produced the first printed copy of the Declaration to include the names of all the signers.

Before reading the Declaration, some colonists hadn't made up their minds. Later, when they read the list of charges against Britain and the king, many agreed independence was their only choice. Some colonists continued to oppose breaking free from Britain. As many as one in three colonists was loyal to the king. Many **Loyalists** were people who had ties to Britain. Government officials depended on Britain too. They knew that, if America won, they would be out of a job.

The first printed version of the Declaration of Independence had only the names of the president and secretary of the Continental Congress.

Britain's response came in action, not words. The king meant to crush the revolution. He sent a powerful armed force against the colonies. Thirty ships arrived on America's shores. They carried 30,000 soldiers, 10,000 sailors, and 1,200 cannons. King George and Parliament sent a message to the world. They weren't going to give up the American colonies easily.

A Long Struggle

The Americans' chances of winning looked bad at the beginning of the war. George Washington, the American leader, was daring and heroic. But his army was made up of untrained farmers and shopkeepers. There was little money to pay his troops or keep them well supplied with food, clothing, and weapons.

The British won most of the battles, but they couldn't win the war. It dragged on. European officers came to help George Washington. Baron von Steuben from Prussia, Poland's Thaddeus Kosciuszko (kos-kee-US-koh), and the Marquis de Lafayette of France volunteered because they believed in liberty. In 1778, the French government, at Benjamin Franklin's urging, sent money, troops, and supplies. In September 1781, Washington's army and the French navy caught the British in a trap. By October 19, the British surrendered.

George Washington

General George Washington was a daring leader who knew he had to take chances to win. On Christmas night, 1776, Washington took his entire army across the Delaware River. In a surprise attack on an enemy camp, the American army took nearly 1,000 prisoners. The victory gave the colonists new hope.

British

Strengths

- ★ More soldiers
- ★ Best trained army in the world
- ★ Experienced officers
- ★ Strongest navy in the world
- ★ More supplies

Weaknesses

- ★ Fighting far from home
- ★ Soldiers less committed to victory

American

Strengths

- ★ Fighting on home soil
- ★ Fighting for a cause
- ★ Leadership of Washington and other officers
- ★ Aid of foreign countries

Weaknesses

- ★ Unprofessional, poorly trained army
- ★ Lack of supplies
- ★ Small navy

Colonists raise an American flag over the Yorktown battlefield.

The Fight Goes On

The Declaration of Independence stated that "all men are created equal." However, the Revolution did not end slavery or give women equal rights.

★

Unfinished Business

It would take almost 90 years before the Civil War would finally end slavery. The struggle of African Americans for full equality would continue long after that.

Salem Poor

Salem Poor was a free black man from Massachusetts. He fought bravely on the American side at the Battle of Bunker Hill in June 1775. After the battle, the American commander described Poor as a "brave and gallant soldier."

Martin Luther King, Jr. marches with his wife and others through Selma, Alabama, in 1965.

The Revolution did not give political equality to American women either. In 1848, Elizabeth Cady Stanton wrote a Declaration of Rights and Sentiments. It began, "We hold these truths to be self-evident; that all men and women are created equal." Stanton's words echoed those of Thomas Jefferson. Stanton had a list of complaints too. She named a great number of rights that men had denied women. Many were the same rights the colonists had fought for 70 years earlier. Still, it took women until 1920 to win the right to vote in national elections.

Women march in Washington, D.C., on the 60th anniversary of winning the right to vote.

Other Revolutions

The success of the American rebels inspired others. Many people in France read the Declaration of Independence. In 1789, French rebels wrote their own Declaration of the Rights of Man and of the Citizen. The French Revolution that followed overthrew the king of France. Between 1795 and 1826, Spanish and French colonies in Latin America won their independence. Since then, the world has seen revolutions in many countries. Not all revolutions have given people equality and independence. To this day, the ideals of the Declaration of Independence continue to live in the minds and hearts of people around the world.

Independence Day

On July 2, 1776, Congress voted in favor of independence from Britain. John Adams wrote to his wife to share the news. He wrote that Americans should mark this day each year as the anniversary of their freedom. Adams wanted them to celebrate with parades, games, bonfires, and lights "from one end of this continent to the other, from this time forward forever more." Adams got the date wrong, as Americans celebrate Congress's July 4 decision to adopt the Declaration of Independence. He was right about how Americans have celebrated their freedom ever since.

Glossary

assembly a lawmaking body

boycott a refusal to deal with or buy goods from someone as a protest

colony a region ruled by another country

Continental Congress the Patriot governing body that signed the Declaration of Independence and formed the American army

Loyalist an American colonist who supported the British king

Parliament Britain's lawmaking body

Patriot an American colonist who favored independence

preamble an introduction to a document

royal governor the person appointed by the king to represent him and approve laws in a colony

subject a person under the authority of a king

tyrant a cruel and unjust ruler

unalienable cannot be taken away

veto reject a proposed law

Jefferson Memorial, Washington, D.C.

The Declaration of Independence

IN CONGRESS, July 4, 1776

The Unanimous Declaration of the Thirteen United States of America

When in the Course of human events, it becomes necessary for one people to dissolve the political bands which have connected them with another, and to assume among the powers of the earth, the separate and equal station to which the Laws of Nature and of Nature's God entitle them, a decent respect to the opinions of mankind requires that they should declare the causes which impel them to the separation.

We hold these truths to be self-evident, that all men are created equal, that they are endowed by their Creator with certain unalienable Rights, that among these are Life, Liberty and the pursuit of Happiness— That to secure these rights, Governments are instituted among Men, deriving their just powers from the consent of the governed, — That whenever any Form of Government becomes destructive of these ends, it is the Right of the People to alter or to abolish it, and to institute new Government, laying its foundation on such principles and organizing its powers in such form, as to them shall seem most likely to effect their Safety and Happiness. Prudence, indeed, will dictate that Governments long established should not be changed for light and transient causes; and

accordingly all experience hath shewn, that mankind are more disposed to suffer, while evils are sufferable, than to right themselves by abolishing the forms to which they are accustomed. But when a long train of abuses and usurpations, pursuing invariably the same Object evinces a design to reduce them under absolute Despotism, it is their right, it is their duty, to throw off such Government, and to provide new Guards for their future security. Such has been the patient sufferance of these Colonies; and such is now the necessity which constrains them to alter their former Systems of Government. The history of the present King of Great Britain is a history of repeated injuries and usurpations, all having in direct object the establishment of an absolute Tyranny over these States. To prove this, let Facts be submitted to a candid world.

He has refused his Assent to Laws, the most wholesome and necessary for the public good.

He has forbidden his Governors to pass Laws of immediate and pressing importance, unless suspended in their operation till his Assent should be obtained; and when so suspended, he has utterly neglected to attend to them.

He has refused to pass other Laws for the accommodation of large districts of people, unless those people would relinquish the right of Representation in the Legislature, a right in-estimable to them and formidable to tyrants only.

He has called together legislative bodies at places unusual, uncomfortable, and distant from the depository of their public Records, for the sole purpose of fatiguing them into compliance with his measures.

He has dissolved Representative Houses repeatedly, for opposing with manly firmness his invasions on the rights of the people.

He has refused for a long time, after such dissolutions, to cause others to be elected; whereby the Legislative powers, incapable of Annihilation, have returned to the People at large for their exercise; the State remaining in the mean time exposed to all the dangers of invasion from without, and convulsions within.

He has endeavoured to prevent the population of these States; for that purpose obstructing the Laws for Naturalization of Foreigners; refusing to pass others to encourage their migrations hither, and raising the conditions of new Appropriations of Lands.

He has obstructed the Administration of Justice, by refusing his Assent to Laws for establishing Judiciary powers.

He has made Judges dependent on his Will alone, for the tenure of their offices, and the amount and payment of their salaries.

He has erected a multitude of New Offices, and sent hither swarms of Officers to harrass our people, and eat out their substance.

He has kept among us, in times of peace, Standing Armies without the Consent of our legislatures.

He has affected to render the Military independent of and superior to the Civil power.

He has combined with others to subject us to a jurisdiction foreign to our constitution, and unacknowledged by our laws; giving his Assent to their Acts of pretended Legislation:

For Quartering large bodies of armed troops among us:

For protecting them, by a mock Trial, from punishment for any Murders which they should commit on the Inhabitants of these States:

For cutting off our Trade with all parts of the world:

For imposing Taxes on us without our Consent:

For depriving us in many cases, of the benefits of Trial by Jury:

For transporting us beyond Seas to be tried for pretended offences:

For abolishing the free System of English Laws in a neighbouring Province, establishing therein an Arbitrary government, and enlarging its Boundaries so as to render it at once an example and fit instrument for introducing the same absolute rule into these Colonies:

For taking away our Charters, abolishing our most valuable Laws, and altering fundamentally the Forms of our Governments:

For suspending our own Legislatures, and declaring themselves invested with power to legislate for us in all cases whatsoever.

He has abdicated Government here, by declaring us out of his Protection and waging War against us.

He has plundered our seas, ravaged our Coasts, burnt our towns, and destroyed the lives of our people.

He is at this time transporting large Armies of foreign Mercenaries to compleat the works of death, desolation and tyranny, already begun with circumstances of Cruelty & perfidy scarcely paralleled in the most barbarous ages, and totally unworthy of the Head of a civilized nation.

He has constrained our fellow Citizens taken Captive on the high Seas to bear Arms against their Country, to become the executioners of their friends and Brethren, or to fall themselves by their Hands.

He has excited domestic insurrections amongst us, and has endeavoured to bring on the inhabitants of our frontiers, the merciless Indian Savages, whose known rule of warfare, is an undistinguished destruction of all ages, sexes and conditions.

In every stage of these Oppressions We have Petitioned for Redress in the most humble terms: Our repeated Petitions have been answered only by repeated injury. A Prince whose character is thus marked by every act which may define a Tyrant, is unfit to be the ruler of a free people.

Nor have We been wanting in attentions to our Brittish brethren. We have warned them from time to time of attempts by their legislature to extend an unwarrantable jurisdiction over us. We have reminded them of the circumstances of our emigration and settlement here. We have appealed to their native justice and magnanimity, and we have conjured them by the ties of our common kindred to disavow these usurpations, which, would inevitably interrupt our connections and correspondence. They too have been deaf to the voice of justice and of consanguinity. We must, therefore, acquiesce in the necessity, which denounces our Separation, and hold them, as we hold the rest of mankind, Enemies in War, in Peace Friends.

We, therefore, the Representatives of the United States of America, in General Congress, Assembled, appealing to the Supreme Judge of the world for the rectitude of our intentions, do, in the Name, and by Authority of the good People of these Colonies, solemnly publish and declare, That these United Colonies are, and of Right ought to be Free and Independent States; that they are Absolved from all Allegiance to the British Crown, and that all political connection between them and the State of Great Britain, is and ought to be totally dissolved; and that as Free and Independent States, they have full Power to levy War, conclude Peace, contract Alliances, establish Commerce, and to do all other Acts and Things which Independent States may of right do. And for the support of this Declaration,

with a firm reliance on the protection of divine Providence, we mutually pledge to each other our Lives, our Fortunes and our sacred Honor.

New Hampshire:
Josiah Bartlett
William Whipple
Matthew Thornton

Massachusetts:
John Hancock
Samuel Adams
John Adams
Robert Treat Paine
Elbridge Gerry

Rhode Island:
Stephen Hopkins
William Ellery

Connecticut:
Roger Sherman
Samuel Huntington
William Williams
Oliver Wolcott

New York:
William Floyd
Philip Livingston
Francis Lewis
Lewis Morris

New Jersey:
Richard Stockton
John Witherspoon
Francis Hopkinson
John Hart
Abraham Clark

Pennsylvania:
Robert Morris
Benjamin Rush
Benjamin Franklin
John Morton
George Clymer
James Smith
George Taylor
James Wilson
George Ross

Delaware:
Caesar Rodney
George Read
Thomas McKean

Maryland:
Samuel Chase
William Paca
Thomas Stone
Charles Carroll of
    Carrollton

Virginia:
George Wythe
Richard Henry Lee
Thomas Jefferson
Benjamin Harrison
Thomas Nelson, Jr.
Francis Lightfoot Lee
Carter Braxton

North Carolina:
William Hooper
Joseph Hewes
John Penn

South Carolina:
Edward Rutledge
Thomas Hayward, Jr.
Thomas Lynch, Jr.
Arthur Middleton

Georgia:
Button Gwinnett
Lyman Hall
George Walton

Source:
The Avalon Project at
Yale Law School
http://www.yale.edu/
lawweb/avalon/declare.htm

Thomas Jefferson's Rough Draft

Note: Blue type below highlights words in Jefferson's draft that differ from those that appear in the final version of the Declaration of Independence.

A Declaration of the Representatives of the UNITED STATES OF AMERICA, in General Congress assembled.

When in the course of human events it becomes necessary for a people to advance from that subordination in which they have hitherto remained, & to assume among the powers of the earth the equal & independant station to which the laws of nature & of nature's god entitle them, a decent respect to the opinions of mankind requires that they should declare the causes which impel them to the change.

We hold these truths to be sacred & undeniable; that all men are created equal & independant, that from that equal creation they derive rights inherent & inalienable, among which are the preservation of life, & liberty, & the pursuit of happiness; that to secure these ends, governments are instituted among men, deriving their just powers from the consent of the governed; that whenever any form of government shall become destructive of these ends, it is the right of the people to alter or to abolish it, & to institute new government, laying it's foundation on such principles & organising it's powers in such form, as to them shall seem most likely to effect their safety & happiness. Prudence indeed will dictate that governments long established should not be changed for light & transient

causes: and accordingly all experience hath shewn that mankind are more disposed to suffer while evils are sufferable, than to right themselves by abolishing the forms to which they are accustomed. But when a long train of abuses & usurpations, begun at a distinguished period, & pursuing invariably the same object, evinces a design to subject them to arbitrary power it is their right, it is their duty, to throw off such government & to provide new guards for their future security. Such has been the patient sufferance of these colonies; & such is now the necessity which constrains them to expunge their former systems of government. The history of his present majesty, is a history of unremitting injuries and usurpations, among which no one fact stands single or solitary to contradict the uniform tenor of the rest, all of which have in direct object the establishment of an absolute tyranny over these states. To prove this, let facts be submitted to a candid world, for the truth of which we pledge a faith yet unsullied by falsehood.

He has refused his assent to laws the most wholesome and necessary for the public good.

He has forbidden his governors to pass laws of immediate & pressing importance, unless suspended in their operation till his assent should be obtained; and when so suspended, he has neglected utterly to attend to them.

He has refused to pass other laws for the accomodation of large districts of people unless those people would relinquish the right of representation, a right inestimable to them, & formidable to tyrants alone.

He has dissolved Representative houses repeatedly & continually, for opposing with manly

35

firmness his invasions on the rights of the people.

He has refused for a long space of time to cause others to be elected, whereby the legislative powers, incapable of annihilation, have returned to the people at large for their exercise, the state remaining in the mean time exposed to all the dangers of invasion from without, & convulsions within.

He has endeavored to prevent the population of these states; for that purpose obstructing the laws for naturalization of foreigners; refusing to pass others to encourage their migrations hither; & raising the conditions of new appropriations of lands.

He has suffered the administration of justice totally to cease in some of these colonies, refusing his assent to laws for establishing judiciary powers.

He has made our judges dependant on his will alone, for the tenure of their offices, and amount of their salaries.

He has erected a multitude of new offices by a self-assumed power, & sent hither swarms of officers to harrass our people & eat out their substance.

He has kept among us in times of peace standing armies & ships of war.

He has affected to render the military, independant of & superior to the civil power.

He has combined with others to subject us to a jurisdiction foreign to our constitutions and unacknowledged by our laws; giving his assent to their pretended acts of legislation, for quartering large bodies of armed troops among us;

for protecting them by a mock-trial from punishment for any murders they should commit on the inhabitants of these states;

for cutting off our trade with all parts of the world;

for imposing taxes on us without our consent;

for depriving us of the benefits of trial by jury;

for transporting us beyond seas to be tried for pretended offences;

for taking away our charters, & altering fundamentally the forms of our governments;

for suspending our own legislatures & declaring themselves invested with power to legislate for us in all cases whatsoever.

He has abdicated government here, withdrawing his governors, & declaring us out of his allegiance & protection.

He has plundered our seas, ravaged our coasts, burnt our towns & destroyed the lives of our people.

He is at this time transporting large armies of foreign mercenaries to compleat the works of death, desolation & tyranny, already begun with circumstances of cruelty & perfidy unworthy the head of a civilized nation.

He has endeavored to bring on the inhabitants of our frontiers the merciless Indian savages, whose known rule of warfare is an undistinguished destruction of all ages, sexes, & conditions of existence.

He has incited treasonable insurrections in our fellow-subjects, with the allurements of forfeiture & confiscation of our property.

He has waged cruel war against human nature itself, violating it's most sacred rights of life & liberty in the persons of a distant people who never offended him, captivating & carrying them into slavery in another hemisphere, or to incur miserable death in their transportation thither. This piratical warfare, the opprobrium of infidel powers, is the warfare of the CHRISTIAN king of Great Britain. Determined to keep open a market where MEN should be bought & sold, he has prostituted his negative for suppressing every legislative attempt to prohibit or to restrain this execrable commerce: and that this assemblage of horrors might want no fact of distinguished die, he is now exciting those very people to rise in arms among us, and to purchase that liberty of which he has deprived them, by murdering the people upon whom he also obtruded them; thus paying off former crimes committed against the liberties of one people, with crimes which he urges them to commit against the lives of another.

In every stage of these oppressions we have petitioned for redress in the most humble terms; our repeated petitions have been answered by repeated injury. A prince whose character is thus marked by every act which may define a tyrant, is unfit to be the ruler of a people who mean to be free. Future ages will scarce believe that the hardiness of one man, adventured within the short compass of 12 years only, on so many acts of tyranny without a mask, over a people fostered & fixed in principles of liberty.

Nor have we been wanting in attentions to our British brethren. We have warned them from time to time of attempts by their legislature to extend a jurisdiction over these our states. We have reminded them of the circumstances of our emigration & settlement here, no one of which could warrant so strange a pretension: that these were effected at the expence of our own blood & treasure, unassisted by the wealth or the strength of Great Britain: that in constituting indeed our several forms of government, we had adopted one common king, thereby laying a foundation for perpetual league & amity with them: but that submission to their parliament was no part of our constitution, nor ever in idea, if history may be credited: and we appealed to their native justice & magnanimity, as well as to the ties of our common kindred to disavow these usurpations which were likely to interrupt our correspond-ence & connection. They too have been deaf to the voice of justice & of consanguinity, & when occasions have been given them, by the regular course of their laws, of removing from their councils the disturbers of our harmony, they have by their free election re-established them in power. at this very time too they are permitting their chief magistrate to send over not only soldiers of our common blood, but Scotch & foreign mercenaries to invade & deluge us in blood. These facts have given the last stab to agonizing affection, and manly spirit bids us to renounce for ever these unfeeling brethren. We must endeavor to forget our former love for them, and to hold them as we hold the rest of mankind, enemies in war, in peace friends. We might have been a free & a great people together; but a communication of grandeur & of freedom it seems is below their dignity. be it so, since they will have it: the road to glory & happiness is open to us too; we will climb it in a separate state, and acquiesce in the necessity which pronounces our everlasting Adieu!

We therefore the representatives of the United States of America in General Congress assembled do, in the name & by authority of the good people of these states, reject and renounce all allegiance & subjection to the kings of Great Britain & all others who may hereafter claim by, through, or under them; we utterly dissolve & break off all political connection which may have heretofore subsisted between us & the people or parliament of Great Britain; and finally we do assert and declare these colonies to be free and independant states, and that as free & independant states they shall hereafter have power to levy war, conclude peace, contract alliances, establish commerce, & to do all other acts and things which independant states may of right do. And for the support of this declaration we mutually pledge to each other our lives, our fortunes, & our sacred honour.

Source: Thomas Jefferson's Papers, Princeton University
http://www.princeton.edu/~tjpapers/declaration/declaration.html

The Constitution of Virginia,

June 29, 1776

The list of grievances against King George III that appeared in the Constitution of Virginia, June 29, 1776, is printed on these pages. This list formed the basis for the one that is included in the Declaration of Independence. The entire text of the Constitution of Virginia is available online at America's Homepage: *http://ahp.gatech.edu/va_constitution_1776.html*

THE CONSTITUTION OR FORM OF G0VERNMENT, AGREED TO AND RESOLVED UPON BY THE DELEGATES AND REPRESENTATIVES OF THE SEVERAL COUNTIES AND CORPORATIONS OF VIRGINIA

Whereas George the third, King of Great Britain and Ireland, and elector of Hanover, heretofore intrusted with the exercise of the kingly office in this government, hath endeavoured to prevent, the same into a detestable and insupportable tyranny, by putting his negative on laws the most wholesome and necessary for the public good:

By denying his Governors permission to pass laws of immediate and pressing importance, unless suspended in their operation for his assent, and, when so suspended neglecting to attend to them for many years:

By refusing to pass certain other laws, unless the persons to be benefited by them would relinquish the inestimable right of representation in the legislature:

By dissolving legislative Assemblies repeatedly and continually, for opposing with manly firmness his invasions of the rights of the people:

When dissolved, by refusing to call others for a long space of time, thereby leaving the political system without any legislative head:

By endeavouring to prevent the population of our country, and, for that purpose, obstructing, the laws for the naturalization of foreigners:

By keeping among us, in times of peace, standing armies and ships of war:

By effecting to render the military independent of, and superior to, the civil power:

By combining with others to subject us to a foreign jurisdiction, giving his assent to their pretended acts of legislation:

For quartering large bodies of armed troops among us:

For cutting off our trade with all parts of the world:

For imposing taxes on us without our consent:

For depriving us of the benefits of trial by jury:

For transporting us beyond seas, to be tried for pretended offences:

For suspending our own legislatures, and declaring themselves invested with power to legislate for us in all cases whatsoever:

By plundering our seas, ravaging our coasts, burning our towns, and destroying the lives of our people:

By inciting insurrections of our fellow subjects, with the allurements of forfeiture and confiscation:

By prompting our negroes to rise in arms against us, those very negroes whom, by an inhuman use of his negative, he hath refused us permission to exclude by law:

By endeavoring to bring on the inhabitants of our frontiers the merciless Indian savages, whose known rule of warfare is an undistinguished destruction of all ages, sexes, and conditions of existence:

By transporting, at this time, a large army of foreign mercenaries, to complete the works of death, desolation, and tyranny, already begun with circumstances of cruelty and perfidy unworthy the head of a civilized nation:

By answering our repeated petitions for redress with a repetition of injuries:

And finally, by abandoning the helm of government and declaring us out of his allegiance and protection.

By which several acts of misrule, the government of this country, as formerly exercised under the crown of Great Britain, is TOTALLY DISSOLVED.

Index